FOURTH EDITION

Great Smoky Mountains

Wildflowers

CARLOS C. CAMPBELL
WILLIAM F. HUTSON
AARON J. SHARP

With additional photographs by David deL. Condon,
Alan S. Heilman, Hershal L. Macon, Ralph M. Sargent,
R. M. Schiele, Jim Thompson, and Ken Thurmond

THE UNIVERSITY OF TENNESSEE PRESS
KNOXVILLE 37996-0325

IMPORTANT NOTICE

Since this flower book was first published, some of the nature trails
have been renamed as follows:

Big Locust is now the Cove Hardwood Nature Trail, pages 10, 16,
18, 20, 24, 28, 32, 36, 40, 44, 52, 82, 96, and 106.

Buckeye Nature Trail is no longer a maintained trail, pages 34, 46,
and 86.

Junglebrook is now the Bud Ogle Nature Trail, pages 40, 56, 80,
and 102.

Pine Oak is now the Cades Cove Nature Trail, pages 34, 46, and 86.

*Appreciation and thanks are expressed to the Great Smoky
Mountains Conservation Association, of Knoxville, for its
substantial assistance in the publication of* GREAT SMOKY
MOUNTAINS WILDFLOWERS. *It was the Conservation Association which in 1924 started the successful movement for
the establishment of the Great Smoky Mountains National
Park, in Tennessee and North Carolina, and which has
continued to work for the best interests of this park.*

The paper in this book meets the minimum requirements of
the American National Standard for Permanence of Paper for
Printed Library Materials. ∞ The binding materials have
been chosen for strength and durability.

THE UNIVERSITY OF TENNESSEE PRESS

L.C. CATALOG CARD #77-126938
ISBN 0–87049–124–5
PRINTED IN THE U.S.A.

STARTING BEFORE THE WINTER'S SNOWS have melted and continuing well into late autumn, there is a gay and colorful procession of wildflowers in the Great Smoky Mountains National Park. The luxuriant, highly varied vegetation of these mountains includes approximately 1,500 species of native flowering herbs, shrubs, and trees. In fact, the park could appropriately be called "The Wildflower National Park." As Arthur Stupka, who for 25 years was Park Naturalist in the Smokies, says, "Vegetation to the Great Smoky Mountains National Park is what granite domes and waterfalls are to Yosemite, geysers are to Yellowstone, and sculptured pinnacles are to Bryce Canyon National Park."

The richness of flora is one of its most distinctive features, the park's diverse environments having provided niches for the survival of many plant species. Situated in one of the oldest mountain masses, the area has not been covered by marine waters nor glacial ice. Here persist a few members of subtropical families which were much better represented in preglacial times. Associated with them are northern types which probably migrated southward during the glacial epoch.

The venerable age of the mountains is only one of several factors which contribute to the great variety of wildflowers and other plant life. Other influences include variations in elevation, rainfall, nature and slope of the rocks, and temperature.

Elevations, for instance, range from 857 feet at the junction of Abrams Creek and Little Tennessee River up to the highest peak in the park, Clingmans Dome at 6,643 feet.

3

Rainfall sometimes exceeds 100 inches a year in the spruce-fir forests on and near the summits. The average for the upper elevations in general is 85 inches, whereas 50 inches a year is more common in the foothills. Thus it is that we find certain types of plants prospering on the drier slopes of the lower elevations and other kinds thriving in the abundant rainfall common to the upper elevations.

Temperatures are influenced by the wide range in elevations. The mountaintops usually are about 10 to 20 degrees cooler than the park foothills. This has an important bearing on the fact that you can find almost as many kinds of flowering plants between the foothills and the peaks as you will see on a trip from the Great Smokies to Canada. Near the summits of several peaks are many species that are common in Canada, such as the yellow-flowered Clinton's lily, wood sorrel, and witch-hobble.

FLOWERS THAT MOVED UP

Nearly all of the flowers the visitor will see in the Great Smokies are native species. Likewise, most of those included in this book are indigenous to the park.

However, there are a few species—usually found in the foothills of the park and in the surrounding valleys—that are now well-established at much higher elevations. Man and nature assisted this upward movement by changing the vegetational cover in some manner, creating what we call "disturbed areas." Man disturbed the cover by removing trees and shrubs from old homesites and in building roads and trails. Nature created other changes with severe windstorms, landslides caused by cloudbursts, and occasionally fires caused by lightning.

It is possible that wind and birds carried seeds of the lowland plants to these fertile disturbed areas at higher elevations. It is more likely, however, that most of the plants "moved up" to their new environment by means of mulching material and grass seeds applied to road banks and shoulders. The disturbed areas, usually quite small in size, may be seen throughout the park, and they have permitted certain beautiful flowers to be found at present locations in unusual abundance. On valley farms, some of the flowers are classed as weeds—a weed being a plant growing where it is not wanted. But, along the high elevation roads and trails the ox-eye daisy, the dandelion, and other such "weeds" are now adding touches of beauty.

FINDING WILDFLOWERS IN THE SMOKIES

A major purpose of this book is to tell *where* and *when* wildflowers may be found *in the Great Smokies*. The desire of the authors is to share with others not only the kaleidoscope of colors and the exquisite form of these flowers but also the thrill of discovery and identification. Such help to flower lovers is not possible in a more general wildflower book, which may treat several areas or even the entire country. Thus, special emphasis has been placed here on filling a unique need for the Smokies visitor by listing easily-found spots where each plant may be seen. In some instances, larger and more conspicuous displays can be found at other locations; but these usually are for the hardier walkers and climbers, who are invited to obtain further information from park naturalists or rangers.

It should be added, too, that the delicate beauty of wildflowers is best revealed at very close range. A discerning eye is more important than miles traveled; frequently, only a short walk from the car is necessary to locate a plant. Many of the flower descriptions are intended to aid the close observer by telling of unusual features to look for.

Although interesting wildflowers may be found in the Great Smokies most of the year, there are two periods of unusual abundance: mid-April to mid-May, and mid-June to mid-July. The annual Wildflower Pilgrimages are held on the last Thursday, Friday, and Saturday of April. Participants have a choice of several trips each day, guided by botanists and other specialists, to areas where many wildflowers may be seen and photographed. Details about the Pilgrimages may be obtained from the Park Naturalist, Sugarlands Visitor Center, Gatlinburg, Tennessee.

The second period of special flowering abundance is

mid-June to mid-July. At this time the extravagant displays of mountain laurel, the rhododendrons, azaleas, and other heath shrubs are massed for the visitor. Park naturalists also conduct frequent hikes and motor caravans to the special displays.

The park's Self-Guiding Nature Trails, a mile or less in length, afford some of the best opportunities for you to find large numbers of wildflowers on your own. Strategically located in a variety of environments, these trails are virtually open-air herbariums.

Two books that deal specifically with the Great Smokies will be helpful to those interested in the flora and natural history of these mountains. One is the Great Smoky Mountains National Park *Natural History Handbook,** written by Mr. Stupka, mentioned earlier. The other is *Mushrooms of the Great Smokies,* a field guide to some mushrooms and their relatives** by L. R. Hesler, nationally-known botanist and former dean of Liberal Arts at The University of Tennessee.

The diversity of the park's flora means, of course, that most of the wildflowers found in these mountains also occur elsewhere. Many grow along the nearby Foothills Parkway and the scenic Blue Ridge Parkway, and on up to Shenandoah National Park. Some will be found in distant sections of the United States and even in other countries, but not necessarily at the same flowering season.

NOTES FOR THE USER OF THIS BOOK

The wildflowers selected for presentation here are representative of the park and surrounding region. The text is designed especially for the layman but is intended to be botanically accurate. For clarity, the word "fruits," as employed by botanists, is used in most cases instead of "berries" or "seeds." Elevation figures are averages based on common occurrence of the plant described, but it is possible to find a few flowers outside the indicated range.

The scientific names used are those found in *Gray's*

---

* National Park Service, Government Printing Office, 1960.

** The University of Tennessee Press, 1960.

Manual of Botany by Fernald, except for *Aster curtissii,*
Geum radiatum, Leiophyllum lyoni, Senecio rugelia, Soli-
dago glomerata, Trillium catesbaei, and *Trillium vaseyi,*
which were obtained from Small's *Manual of the South-*
eastern Flora. For a more technical treatment of our wildflowers these two texts will be helpful, as will *Britton &*
Brown's Illustrated Flora by Gleason, and other texts.

The various flowers are grouped roughly in the order
of their blooming season. With two enlargements of the
book, however, it became impractical to maintain a strict
chronological grouping. Thus, you will find a few early
species at or near the back of the book along with plants
with late flowers or especially beautiful fruits. Such mis-
placed plants include trout lily, doll's eyes, hairy buttercup, and umbrella magnolia.

Park regulations must be observed along the 500 miles
of park trails. Within the Great Smoky Mountains National Park anyone who picks, digs, or breaks any wildflower (or disturbs animal life) is subject to arrest. Strict
adherence to the law will ensure an unspoiled mountain
scene for all generations to enjoy.

It is our hope that the following camera and word pic-
tures will help to enrich your visit to the Great Smoky
Mountains National Park.

—The Authors

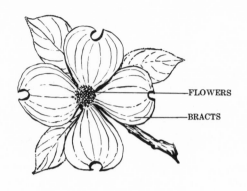

FLOWERS

BRACTS

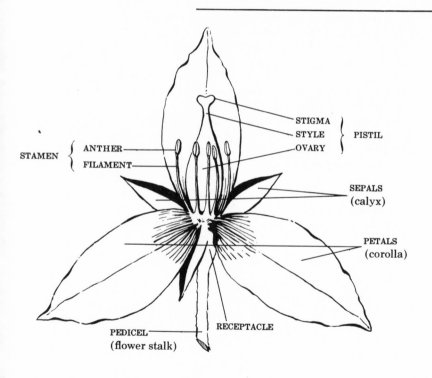

STIGMA
STYLE   PISTIL
OVARY

STAMEN { ANTHER
           FILAMENT

SEPALS
(calyx)

PETALS
(corolla)

PEDICEL
(flower stalk)

RECEPTACLE

FLOWERS AND INFLORESCENCES

A flower as seen by a botanist is really a short stem terminated by whorls of modified leaves. The outermost set of "leaves" (the calyx) consists of sepals usually green in color. The next whorl above consists of petals (collectively the corolla) usually white or colored some shade other than green. Between the corolla and the pistil(s) are the stamens, each consisting of a filament, often erect, terminated by a head-like anther containing pollen. The tip (stigma) of the pistil is the part receptive to the pollen. It is apical on a stalk (style) which is borne on top of the ovary, the enlarged basal portion of the pistil, which may mature into a fruit. Within the fruits the seeds develop. All of the flower parts are attached to the apex (receptacle) of a stem (pedicel).

At times it is difficult to distinguish between a flower and a cluster (inflorescence) of flowers. In the flowering dogwood (see drawing at left) a group of small, inconspicuous flowers are surrounded by four large, white, special leaves (bracts). In the sunflower, small flowers in the center of the head are surrounded by much larger and more showy ray-flowers around the edge. In such instances, what appears to be a single flower is in reality a whole corsage, or bouquet.

TRAILING ARBUTUS   *Epigaea repens*
Heath family

This dwarf shrub is fairly common in sandy, acid soils from 1,000 to 4,000 feet elevation in the Great Smokies. It may be seen along the trail to Abrams Falls and is found on Andrews Bald (5,800 feet) and occasionally at other high elevations. All plants are protected by federal law in the Smokies and other national parks, but trailing arbutus is one of several plants also protected by law in many states. The delicately scented white to pink flowers appear from early March through May. Its rare beauty has been heralded by some of our early poets.

HEPATICA   *Hepatica acutiloba*
Buttercup family

The acute-leaved hepatica is one of two species of the genus which adorns the trailsides in the lower elevations, and occurs up to 3,000 feet. The average height is 3 or 4 inches. Its flowers range from pure white through the pinks, blues, and purples. Exceptionally fine displays may be seen on the Big Locust Nature Trail during March and April, depending on whether spring is early or late. Because of the shape of the hepatica leaf, people in the Middle Ages regarded it as a cure for liver ailments. The other species is *Hepatica americana.*

SPRING BEAUTY   *Claytonia virginica*
Purslane family

With dainty and beautiful flowers, the spring beauty is fairly abundant at all elevations in the Smokies. It is one of the earliest to bloom—usually from late February through May. The narrow-leaved plants are frequently found mixed with the broad-leaved type and many intermediate forms. Only 3 or 4 inches tall, spring beauty grows on rich, wooded slopes. A good place to find it is along the Appalachian Trail between Newfound Gap and Indian Gap.

Trailing Arbutus

Macon photo

Hepatica

Heilman photo

Spring Beauty

Macon photo

UMBRELLA-LEAF
Diphylleia cymosa
Barberry family

Related to may-apple, this perennial herb is occasionally more than 24 inches tall. The relatively small white flowers appear above the leaves in April and May. Its favorite habitat is very wet, rocky slopes, usually in deep shade, at elevations from 2,500 to 6,000 feet. Rather rare and restricted to the Southern Appalachians, umbrella-leaf may be found near Rainbow Falls and alongside the highway below Chimneys Picnic Area. An almost identical sister species occurs in the Alps of Japan.

SQUAW-ROOT
Conopholis americana
Broom-rape family

This parasite, growing on oak roots, is also known as CANCER-ROOT and SQUAW-CORN. Ranging in height from 4 to 9 inches, the brown-colored plant, without chlorophyll, resembles a slender pine cone or a small ear of corn. It is rather uncommon, although widely distributed in oak forests below 4,500 feet elevation. Squaw-root may be seen in late April and May along the Laurel Falls Trail.

STONECROP
Sedum ternatum
Orpine family

The small white flowers, on fleshy plants from 4 to 5 inches tall and with whorled, ovate leaves, appear in April and May. The habitat is moss-covered boulders and bluffs and stream banks at elevations up to 2,500 feet. It may be seen along the Huskey Gap Trail and in Little River Gorge. The genus name, *Sedum*, is also used as a common name by many people. This is the only native *Sedum* in the Smokies, but there are two introduced species, *S. acre* and *S. telephium*.

Umbrella Leaf
Thompson photo

Squaw-root
Sargent photo

Stonecrop
Hutson photo

BIRDFOOT VIOLET

Viola pedata var. *lineariloba*

Violet family

This is one of 31 violets in the Great Smokies. Unlike the original birdfoot violet that has 2 dark and 3 lighter petals, all 5 petals of this variety are bluish-purple. It blooms from March through June, and is identified by the leaves, which somewhat resemble the shape of a bird's foot. A favorite habitat for this violet is the dry, open woods, especially along park trails and roads, such as the Rich Mountain Road, between 900 and 3,000 feet elevation.

LONGSPUR VIOLET

Viola rostrata

Violet family

This distinctively shaped violet with a long, slender spur is usually blue but sometimes white. Found on moist, wooded slopes at elevations of 1,000 to 3,500 feet, it blooms through April and May. The longspur violet is closely related to *V. conspersa*. Neither species is common in the Smokies, but the former may be found along the road to Greenbrier.

SWEET WHITE VIOLET

Viola blanda

Violet family

One of three white violets often confused, this one is abundant in the foothills of the Smokies. At elevations of 4,000 to 5,000 feet it may be found along with *V. pallens*. The third white species, *V. incognita*, is found in lower elevations, but is rare. They grow in moist to wet, shaded, acid soils and bloom from March through June, along almost any brook above 2,500 feet elevation.

Birdfoot Violet
Macon photo

Longspur Violet
Hutson photo

Sweet White Violet
Macon photo

BISHOP'S CAP
Saxifrage family

Mitella diphylla

The creamy white flowers, appearing as tiny fringed bells when viewed under a lens, cling closely to the upper half of the 10 to 15-inch stems. They appear in April and May at elevations up to 2,500 feet and may be seen in Little River Gorge. The favorite habitat is moist, rich wooded slopes and stream banks. MITERWORT is another common name.

TOOTHWORT
Mustard family

Dentaria diphylla

The white to pink or purple flowers, on stems from 8 to 10 inches tall, appear in April and May. Fairly common along park trails and roads and on rich wooded slopes at elevations up to 3,500 feet, toothwort is easily found in Little River Gorge. Also known as PEPPERROOT because of the acrid rootstock, this is one of the wild "salads" called creases or cresses by mountain people.

WHORLED POGONIA
Orchid family

Isotria verticillata

This interesting but extremely rare orchid, also known as FIVE-LEAVED ORCHID, is found in only a few scattered pine-oak forests in the Smokies. The plant, reaching a height of 8 to 16 inches, sometimes grows near pink lady's-slipper. It is seen in April and May.

WILD GINGER
Birthwort family

Asarum acuminatum

The heart-shaped leaves of this ginger species last only one season in contrast to the evergreen leaves of *A. arifolium*. The meaty, jug-like flowers have three long, slender, flaring sepals but no petals. It is fairly abundant on rich slopes along streams at elevations up to 3,000 feet. The unusual brown flowers appearing in April and May may be seen near post #11 on the Big Locust Nature Trail. It is related to *A. canadense*, which has shorter and much more obtuse sepals.

Bishop's Cap   *Hutson photo*

Toothwort   *Hutson photo*

Whorled Pogonia   *Heilman photo*

Wild Ginger   *Hutson photo*

BLUE COHOSH   *Caulophyllum thalictroides*
      Barberry family

The yellowish-green flowers, on plants about 2 feet tall, appear in late April and May. Fairly common on rich woodlands up to about 3,000 feet elevation, they may be seen on the Big Locust Nature Trail. An unusual feature is that the fast-growing seed ruptures its green fruit-covering, which remains below the blue, spherical seed at maturity. Other common names are ELECTRIC LIGHT BULB PLANT and PAPOOSE-ROOT. This plant is not related to the black cohosh, also common in the Smokies.

LOUSEWORT   *Pedicularis canadensis*
      Figwort family

If you find the name "lousewort" to be somewhat offensive, you may call it WOOD-BETONY. People once believed that cattle would become infested with lice upon touching this plant. The pale yellow to reddish-brown flowers appear in April and May on stems 8 to 12 inches tall. The leaves are fern-like. It occurs up to 3,500 feet elevation and may be seen in abundance along the Buckeye Nature Trail. The plant is often partially parasitic, being attached to roots of other plants.

BLOODROOT   *Sanguinaria canadensis*
      Poppy family

This is one of the very early wildflowers, appearing from mid-March to mid-April. The clear white flowers, on stems about 8 inches tall, grow along the Big Locust Nature Trail, the Roaring Fork Motor Nature Trail, and generally in moist, deciduous woods up to about 3,000 feet. The slender, oval petals normally drop off in one to three days. Interestingly, the flower stem rises through an open space at the base of the accompanying leaf; also, the root contains an orange-red sap, which accounts for the common name.

Blue Cohosh

Hutson photo

Lousewort

Hutson photo

Bloodroot

Macon photo

DUTCHMAN'S-PIPE — *Aristolochia durior*
Birthwort family

This climbing vine gets its name from the similarity of the flower's shape to that of the traditional pipe of the Dutch. It is fairly common in the moist woods of the Smokies up to about 4,000 feet, but the flowers which appear in April and May are seldom seen because of their greenish color and because so many of them bloom high in the trees. The species may be seen along the Buckeye Nature Trail.

MAY-APPLE — *Podophyllum peltatum*
Barberry family

Also known as MANDRAKE, this plant is 10 to 18 inches tall and has two prominent peltate leaves. A single inconspicuous flower appears in May near the junction of the leaf stalks. Colonies of 50 to 100 or more plants grow in open woods and on road shoulders up to 2,500 feet and are easily recognized along the Big Locust Nature Trail.

FOAMFLOWER — *Tiarella cordifolia*
Saxifrage family

The white to creamy-white flowers, on stems 8 to 10 inches tall, appear in April and May. They are rather common on rich, wooded slopes up to about 4,000 feet elevation and may be seen along the Sugarlands Nature Trail and near Deep Creek Campground.

CREEPING PHLOX — *Phlox stolonifera*
Phlox family

Sizable spots of bright color ranging from blue to pink-purple, seen along park roads in April and May, are likely to be creeping phlox. It is 8 to 10 inches tall and is found along the Buckeye Nature Trail and elsewhere from 1,000 to 3,500 feet elevation. The creeping is done by stolons; hence the species name.

Dutchman's-pipe   *Hutson photo*

May-apple   *Hutson photo*

Foamflower   *Hutson photo*

Creeping Phlox   *Hutson photo*

STRIPED MAPLE
Acer pensylvanicum
Maple family

One of 7 maples in the Smokies, this tree, usually less than
35 feet tall, has green bark, striped with white, and light
green flowers. Found from 1,000 to 3,500 feet elevation, it
flowers on Cades Cove Vista Trail in late April and May.
Other common names include PENNSYLVANIA MAPLE,
MOOSEWOOD, and GOOSEFOOT MAPLE.

MOUNTAIN MAPLE
Acer spicatum
Maple family

Fairly common on moist, wooded slopes at elevations from
3,000 to 6,500 feet, this small tree with a shrubby appearance has erect, light green spikes of flowers and slightly
wrinkled leaves. It may be seen along the road banks near
Indian Gap from May into July.

PRINCESS TREE
Paulownia tomentosa
Figwort family

Native to Asia, this fast-growing tree apparently is well
established in the Smokies at elevations up to 2,500 feet.
Known locally as EMPRESS TREE, it is found along Little
River below Elkmont. The flowers appear in late April
and early May before the opposite leaves, which resemble
the whorled *Catalpa* leaves. The Japanese prize the wood
above all others, using it to make watertight boxes for
storing valuable possessions. Often the tree is planted at
a daughter's birth, for her dowry.

POISON IVY
Rhus radicans
Cashew family

Immediate recognition of this clinging vine is a must for
every hiker in the park. Few people are immune, even
temporarily, from poisoning upon contact with any part
of the plant (dead or alive), including its pollen or even
smoke when burned. The 3 leaflets distinguish it from the
5's of the non-poisonous Virginia creeper. Poison ivy's
small, greenish flowers appear from May to July, followed
by fruits which are enjoyed by some birds.

(left)
Striped Maple
Hutson photo

(right)
Mountain Maple
Hutson photo

Princess Tree
Hutson photo

Poison Ivy
Schiele photo

COLUMBINE
Aquilegia canadensis
Buttercup family

With strikingly beautiful flowers, the wild columbine presents an elegant show, as along the lower portion of Little River Gorge. It is fairly common throughout April and early May. Abundant at elevations of 900 to 2,500 feet, the columbine also is seen occasionally at much higher elevations, such as at Mile High where it blooms in early summer. Usually 18 to 24 inches high, the plant is especially attractive against a background of a rock cliff or the foamy water of a nearby stream.

FIRE PINK
Silene virginica
Pink family

The scarlet fire pink, about a foot tall, is usually found on dry, steep banks along roads and trails at elevations of 1,500 to 2,500 feet. It is seen in April at the lower elevations, but as late as May and June at higher levels. Little River Gorge is a good place to look for fire pink, which is a relative of starry campion and three other *Silene* species in the Smokies.

SMOOTH YELLOW VIOLET
Viola pensylvanica
Violet family

Also known as PENNSYLVANIA VIOLET, this species is quite common in deciduous woods that are moist but well drained. Flowers appear in April and early May. The height ranges from 4 to 15 inches, depending on the fertility of the soil. It is widely distributed at elevations below 2,500 feet, but may be seen on the Big Locust Nature Trail.

GAY WINGS
Polygala paucifolia
Milkwort family

Only 3 to 4 inches tall, this perennial herb is rare in the Smokies. It has been found along the trail to Abrams Falls and near the first ford on the Cades Cove Loop Road. The attractive orchid-pink flowers, shown three times actual size, are seen in April. It is also known as FRINGED POLYGALA and BIRD-ON-THE-WING.

Columbine — *Hutson photo*

Fire Pink — *Hutson photo*

Smooth Yellow Violet — *Hutson photo*

Gay Wings — *Schiele photo*

ALTERNATE-LEAVED DOGWOOD
Cornus alternifolia

Dogwood family

Also known as PAGODA DOGWOOD (because of its peculiar branching) and GREEN OSIER, one of these small trees is located on the main road opposite Park Headquarters. Showy clusters of white flowers, without large bracts, are found in April and May at lower elevations but appear somewhat later higher up. Fruits of this dogwood are blue, in contrast to the bright red ones of *C. florida*.

BLACKBERRY
Rubus species

Rose family

Flourishing at all elevations, the many species of blackberry are important as wildlife food and ground cover in the Smokies. Blackberries are among the first plants to become established after forest fires, "blow-downs," or other disturbances. The woody arching canes reach a height of 4 to 8 feet the first year, bear flowers and fruit the second year, and then die, remaining upright for another year or so. After early summer flowering, fruits ripen from early July through August, depending upon the elevation. Canes of *R. canadensis*, a species common at higher elevations, have few spines or thorns.

WILD STRAWBERRY
Fragaria virginiana

Rose family

The white flowers appear in April and May on plants 6-7 inches tall, which spread by runners and have "three-fingered" leaves. Delicious red fruits start maturing in June along roads and trailsides at lower elevations, such as near Fightin' Creek Gap, and in August at higher levels, as on Parsons Bald (4,700 feet).

COMMON CINQUEFOIL
Potentilla canadensis

Rose family

Also known as FIVE-FINGERS, this yellow-flowered plant resembles wild strawberry except for flower color and number of leaflets. Flowers appear in May and June, followed by inconspicuous dry fruits. They may be seen, along with wild strawberries, on road shoulders near Fightin' Creek Gap.

Alternate-leaved Dogwood

Hutson photo

(left) Blackberry

Hutson photo

(right) Wild Strawberry

Hutson photo

Common Cinquefoil

Hutson photo

DUTCHMAN'S-BREECHES   *Dicentra cucullaria*
Fumitory family

This distinctively shaped nodding flower, with spurs at the top, is found from 900 to 5,000 feet elevation in the Smokies, but is rather rare. Because of the extended "trouser legs," it is sometimes called LITTLE BOY PLANT. The cream-white flowers appear in April and May, and may be found along the Big Locust Nature Trail.

SQUIRREL CORN   *Dicentra canadensis*
Fumitory family

Very closely related to dutchman's-breeches, this plant has the same elevational range and blooming season. Because of the rounded or "bloomer-like" top of its flowers, it is occasionally called LITTLE GIRL PLANT. Squirrel corn gets its name from a belief that squirrels enjoy its corn-like tubers.

BLEEDING HEART   *Dicentra eximia*
Fumitory family

This beautiful wildflower, rare in the Smokies, grows approximately 12 inches tall. Its habitat is moist bluffs along stream banks at elevations of 1,000 to 2,500 feet, particularly along Little River Gorge. Its flower is a pink version of the related squirrel corn, but bleeding heart is taller. It blooms in May.

PURPLE PHACELIA   *Phacelia bipinnatifida*
Waterleaf family

Reaching a height of 12 to 24 inches, this is the tallest of the three phacelias in the Smokies. Purple phacelia blooms in April and May. It is found in some abundance, with columbines, in Little River Gorge and along park roads and trails from the valleys up to 2,000 feet elevation.

(left)
Dutchman's-breeches

Hutson photo

(right)
Squirrel Corn

Macon photo

Bleeding Heart

Hutson photo

Purple Phacelia

Macon photo

BLACK CHERRY
Prunus serotina

Rose family

At elevations up to 4,500 feet, many of these large trees reach diameters of 36 to 52 inches, formerly serving as lumber for valuable furniture. Flowers, appearing in May and June, may be seen along the road below Newfound Gap. So many of these trees occur below Ramsey Cascades that early settlers called the area "the cherry orchard." Another species, choke cherry, is known to grow only near the Buckeye Nature Trail.

STAR GRASS
Hypoxis hirsuta

Amaryllis family

Except for the difference in leaf arrangement and flower color, this small plant somewhat resembles blue-eyed grass and belongs to a closely related plant family. Leaves are in two rows in blue-eyed grass and in spirals in star grass. The latter may be found along the Laurel Falls Trail in late April and May.

BLUE-EYED GRASS
Sisyrinchium angustifolium

Iris family

These small blue flowers appear on flattened grass-like stems up to 8 inches tall. They are locally abundant in Little River Gorge in May and near Mile High in June and July.

YELLOW BUCKEYE
Aesculus octandra

Buckeye family

This large tree may be identified by the scaly bark, compound leaf with five large leaflets, clusters of yellow flowers at the ends of branches, and fruits (buckeyes) less prickly than those of many other buckeyes. The flowers may be seen in May and June along park roads up to elevations of 4,000 feet. Because the wood does not split easily, it was much used by mountain people for making butter bowls and other utensils. Many people carry a buckeye as a "good luck charm."

Black Cherry

Hutson photo

**(left)
Star Grass**

Hutson photo

**(right)
Blue-eyed Grass**

Hutson photo

Yellow Buckeye

Sargent photo

INDIAN-PINK
Spigelia marilandica

Logania family

This plant, 15 to 20 inches in height and rare in the Great Smokies, occurs only in limestone soils around the edges of the park. Its flowers may be seen on the Rich Mountain Road near the park border in May and June. The slender trumpet-shaped flowers are red on the outside, with a clear yellow on the inside or throat of the trumpet. The logania family, which is the source of strychnine, has no other species in the Southern Appalachians.

GREAT CHICKWEED
Stellaria pubera var. *silvatica*

Pink family

Five white petals, often mistaken for ten petals because each petal is so deeply cleft, give a star-like appearance to this wildflower. A close look reveals tiny black balls or anthers at the tips of the stamens. The flowers appear in April and May, on stems 6 to 8 inches tall. Common on wooded slopes and roadsides up to 4,000 feet elevation, the plant is found along Smokemont and Big Locust Nature Trails.

LARGE-FLOWERED TRILLIUM
Trillium grandiflorum

Lily family

Perhaps the most abundant of the 10 *Trilliums* of the Great Smokies, this is also one of the most beautiful. The big, bell-shaped white flower, which usually turns to a delicate pink with age, is on a stem 10 to 15 inches high and appears in April and May. The habitat is wooded slopes from 1,000 to 3,500 feet elevation. Considerable quantities grow in the vicinity of Chimneys Picnic Area. The yellow center of this *Trillium* helps distinguish it from the erect white variety of *T. erectum* (shown on the back cover), which has a dark, and occasionally white, center.

Indian-pink

Sharp photo

Great Chickweed

Hutson photo

Large-flowered Trillium

Hutson photo

GOLDEN RAGWORT
Senecio aureus
Composite family

The conspicuous yellow flower-heads, on plants 15 to 25 inches tall, are common from April through July in moist soil below 2,500 feet in the park and along roads in the surrounding region.

CATESBY'S TRILLIUM
Trillium catesbaei
Lily family

The white pendant flowers, on stems 10 to 12 inches tall, appear in May. Some petals turn pink with age, but a few are pink from the first. Although a rare species, limited to the Southern Appalachians, several plants may be seen along the Pine-Oak Nature Trail. Unlike most wildflowers, it takes six years for a *Trillium* to flower.

SPANISH BAYONET
Yucca smalliana
Lily family

Known as Spanish bayonet because of its tough, sword-shaped leaves, it is also one of several plants commonly called BEARGRASS. Numerous creamy white flowers, 1 to 1½ inches in diameter, occur on branches of the 4 to 6-foot stem in late May and June. Although widely distributed in thin, rocky soil of the lower elevations, only a few plants grow at each location. It may be seen in Little River Gorge. Many botanists insist that this is *Y. flaccida*.

VASEY'S TRILLIUM
Trillium vaseyi
Lily family

This *Trillium* has the largest flower of all species, often nearly 4 inches in diameter. The dark maroon-purple flowers hanging below the leaves appear on plants up to 30 inches tall from May to early July. Although limited to the Southern Appalachians and generally rare in the Smokies, it is locally rather abundant in a few moist, deep-shaded locations below 3,500 feet, such as between Chero-kee Orchard and Rainbow Falls.

Golden Ragwort   *Hutson photo*

Catesby's Trillium   *Hutson photo*

Spanish Bayonet   *Hutson photo*

Vasey's Trillium   *Thompson photo*

YELLOW TRILLIUM   *Trillium luteum*
Lily family

Three leaves, three petals, and three sepals characterize
the trillium genus. This lemon-scented species, growing to
a height of 8 to 12 inches, is a prominent spring flower
up to about 3,000 feet elevation in the Smokies. It may be
seen on the Big Locust, Buckeye, and Smokemont Nature
Trails, where it blooms in April and May. A closely related species, Huger's trillium, has brownish-purple petals
and a slightly unpleasant odor.

PAINTED TRILLIUM   *Trillium undulatum*
Lily family

One of the 10 trilliums (8 species and 2 varieties) of the
Great Smokies, the painted trillium is found on moist,
shaded slopes from 3,000 to 6,500 feet elevation. It reaches
a height of 8 to 12 inches and blooms in April and May.
The "painted" part of the name refers to the pink "V" at
the base of the white petals. This trillium may be seen
on Clingmans Dome and Mt. Le Conte.

CRESTED DWARF IRIS   *Iris cristata*
Iris family

Widely distributed at lower elevations of the Smokies, this
beautiful iris does much to brighten the roadsides during
April and May. The flower is usually a rich blue, but occasionally a light purple or even white. It is 4 to 6 inches
tall and is found mostly on open slopes. *I. verna* is the
only other species in the park. Iris is the Tennessee State
Flower. Look for the native species in Little River Gorge.

Yellow Trillium

Hutson photo

Painted Trillium

Hutson photo

Crested Dwarf Iris

Hutson photo

FLOWERING DOGWOOD   *Cornus florida*
Dogwood family

This popular small tree, found at elevations up to 3,500 feet, is noted for its profusion of blooms, its rich foliage, and its bright red fruits. The actual flowers, not open in this picture, are small, green, and centrally located. They are surrounded by showy white bracts that most laymen erroneously think are the petals. The foliage, dark green in summer and rich red in autumn, almost excels the beauty of the flowering tree. Flowers appear in April and May, with fruits maturing in September, and the leaves coloring in October. Two other species occur in the park. Flowering dogwood is the North Carolina State Flower. It may be found "almost anywhere" below 3,000 feet.

REDBUD   *Cercis canadensis*
Legume family

In early spring the deep pink flowers of the redbud do much to brighten the landscape up to about 1,500 feet elevation. The tree is unusual in that the flowers, which come in April and May, often appear directly from the trunk, as well as from the branches. JUDAS TREE is another common name, because it is said that Judas hanged himself from a redbud tree. Exceptionally fine displays of redbud may be seen in Little River Gorge.

SOURWOOD   *Oxydendrum arboreum*
Heath family

This small tree is conspicuous for its graceful sprays of white flowers from June to August and for the extreme brilliance of its red leaves in autumn. It is abundant up to about 3,500 feet. The pale gray fruits, which remain through the summer, are often mistaken for flowers. It is our only member of the heath family that is truly a tree. The nectar from its flowers produces the choicest of all wild honey. Sourwoods may be seen on the lawn of the Sugarlands Visitor Center.

Flowering Dogwood

Hutson photo

Redbud

Hutson photo

Sourwood

Hutson photo

YELLOWWOOD   *Cladrastis lutea*
Pulse family

This somewhat rare tree, with large clusters of flowers hanging gracefully from its branches, is a thing of beauty in June. It is thinly scattered at elevations from 1,500 to 3,500 feet and may be seen at the roadside vantage point just above Huskey Gap Trail, and on Junglebrook and Big Locust Nature Trails. The leaves and flowers, with their white corollas, resemble wisteria. Other common names are CHITTUM and GOPHERWOOD, which legend tells us was used by Noah in building his ark. Early settlers obtained yellow dye from the wood.

TULIP TREE   *Liriodendron tulipifera*
Magnolia family

Although frequently called YELLOW POPLAR, or just POPLAR, this big tree of the Smokies is related to the magnolia and is not a true poplar. Sometimes reaching a diameter of 6 feet, it is quite abundant at elevations up to 3,500 feet. The nearest relative is in eastern Asia. Fine examples of this tree may be seen along Ramsey Cascades Trail and on the first two miles of Gregory Ridge Trail. The tulip-shaped flowers open in May and June.

BLACK LOCUST   *Robinia pseudo-acacia*
Pulse family

Loaded with clusters of white flowers, these plentiful trees make an attractive display on the mountainsides below 3,000 feet elevation in April and May. They are especially noticeable in the Sugarlands between park headquarters and Chimney Tops. The nation's second largest black locust—52 inches in diameter—is a major feature of the Big Locust Nature Trail.

Yellowwood

Condon photo

Tulip Tree

Hutson photo

Black Locust

Schiele photo

PINK LADY'S-SLIPPER   *Cypripedium acaule*
Orchid family

Generally rare, this orchid is locally abundant in a few Great Smokies' locations below 3,000 feet. The stately pink flower with curled brown sepals appears at the top of a leafless stalk 12 to 18 inches in height. There are two basal leaves. It is also known as PINK MOCCASIN FLOWER and may be seen in April and May near the end of the Cades Cove Vista Nature Trail.

FLAME AZALEA   *Rhododendron calendulaceum*
Heath family

The highly popular flame azalea occurs as scattered plants and small groups throughout the park. It flowers from April to July, depending on elevation. Fine displays may be seen on Andrews Bald and near Mile High in late June. Dramatic masses of hybrid azaleas, with colors ranging from white to red, are seen on Gregory Bald in late June and early July. Although essentially a deciduous *Rhododendron,* the azalea is known to mountain people as WILD HONEYSUCKLE.

WHITE FRINGED PHACELIA   *Phacelia fimbriata*
Waterleaf family

Only 3 to 5 inches tall, this *Phacelia* is noted for massing in large beds, sometimes covering almost an acre. From a distance, the beds resemble patches of snow. The plant is widely distributed at elevations from 2,500 to 5,000 feet and blooms in April and May. An easily accessible location for viewing is the entrance to Chimneys Picnic Area. Many visitors see only the "snow," but those who take time to really examine this exquisite flower are rewarded by the rare beauty depicted in the accompanying close-up picture.

Pink Lady's-slipper   *Hutson photo*

Flame Azalea   *Hutson photo*

Mass of Phacelia   *Hutson photo*

Close-up of Phacelia   *Heilman photo*

YELLOW BEAD LILY   *Clintonia borealis*
Lily family

This small lily in the high Smokies has abundant small, greenish-yellow flowers in May and early June hanging gracefully from stems 8 to 12 inches high. Yellow bead lily has only basal leaves. The Spruce-Fir Nature Trail and the Clingmans Dome Road in the vicinity of Mt. Collins are good places to see these plants. For a related species, see Clinton's lily (*C. umbellulata*), p. 54.

PINXTER-FLOWER   *Rhododendron nudiflorum*
Heath family

This shrub, also known as PURPLE HONEYSUCKLE, grows 4 to 8 feet tall. Because of the shape of its flowers, which open from mid-April to mid-May, it often is confused with honeysuckle. Pinxter-flower is widely scattered, but not rare, in open woodlands at lower park elevations, and may be seen along the road to Cherokee Orchard.

CANADA VIOLET   *Viola canadensis*
Violet family

Canada violet is the tallest of the park's 31 species, with a stem from 10 to 12 inches tall. Its white flowers, fading later to a pale blue or light purple, are seen from April to June at elevations up to 4,000 feet. It is widely distributed on rich, wooded slopes, and may be found in abundance along the Big Locust Nature Trail.

BLUE HAW   *Viburnum cassinoides*
Honeysuckle family

One of the eight *Viburnum* species in the Great Smokies is a 10-foot shrub fairly abundant at elevations up to 6,000 feet. It may be seen on Andrews Bald. The white flowers appear in June, with fruits maturing in August and September. Other common names include WILD RAISIN and ARROW-WOOD. The red haw (*Crataegus*) is not related.

Yellow Bead Lily   *Hutson photo*

Pinxter-flower   *Sargent photo*

Canada Violet   *Hutson photo*

Blue Haw   *Hutson photo*

SHOWY ORCHIS
Orchis spectabilis

Orchid family

With a combination of white and pink to lavender petals, this is regarded by many as the prettiest of the 29 orchids of the Great Smokies. It is rather rare, usually occurring as only two or three clusters of four or five plants each. Occasionally, however, there will be a score or more such clusters in a radius of 100 feet. The flowers, on stems 6 to 8 inches tall, appear in April and May in moist, wooded areas with loamy soil at elevations of 1,500 to 3,000 feet. Showy orchis may be seen near the Sugarlands Visitor Center and along the Cosby Nature Trail.

BUSH HONEYSUCKLE
Diervilla sessilifolia

Honeysuckle family

This low-growing shrub, only 3 or 4 feet tall, is rather common in forest openings or exposed ridges at the higher elevations of the Smokies and nearby mountains, such as along the famous Appalachian Trail. The yellow flowers are present from late June through August. The leafblades have no leafstalk and are attached directly to the shrub's branches.

YELLOW LADY'S-SLIPPER
Cypripedium calceolus

Orchid family

With its yellow "moccasin" and slightly curled brown sepals, this orchid has a scattered distribution in the Smokies. Growing on moist, rich slopes from 900 to 3,000 feet, it reaches a height of 12 to 18 inches. It blooms in May. A relative, the pink lady's-slipper (*C. acaule*), is locally more abundant, found in large patches along the Vista Nature Trail, but still rare. A difference, other than color, is that the pink species has only two basal leaves. Both species are also known as MOCCASIN FLOWER. The yellow species grows along the Roaring Fork Motor Nature Trail.

Showy Orchis

Hutson photo

Bush Honeysuckle

Hutson photo

**Yellow
Lady's-slipper**

Hutson photo

MOUNTAIN MYRTLE   *Leiophyllum lyoni*
Heath family

This small shrub is restricted mainly to the edges of laurel slicks from 4,000 to 6,500 feet elevation in the Smokies. The star-like flowers, ranging from white to pale pink, appear mostly in June but sometimes earlier. The plant, only 15 to 20 inches tall, grows in dense beds. Myrtle Point on Mt. Le Conte was named for this beautiful shrub.

WITCH-HOBBLE   *Viburnum alnifolium*
Honeysuckle family

Although sometimes found at intermediate elevations, witch-hobble is particularly abundant in the moist, rich, shaded soils of the spruce-fir forests. The large white, marginal flowers surrounding the smaller central blossoms make a fine display in late April and May. The bright red fruits and the beautifully colored leaves of late August through October are equally attractive. The plant is seen to good advantage along the Spruce-Fir Nature Trail. This shrub, growing to a height of 6 to 10 feet, is one of eight *Viburnum* species of the park.

SILVERBELL   *Halesia carolina*
Storax family

Small white, bell-shaped flowers hang from the branches of this small to medium-sized tree. It is abundant in rich, loamy, shaded soils from 900 to 5,000 feet elevation in the Smokies. Excellent displays may be seen in April and May along the Newfound Gap Highway (U.S. 441) on both sides of the mountain. PEAWOOD is another common name.

Mountain Myrtle

Hutson photo

Witch-hobble

Macon photo

Silverbell

Sharp photo

FAIRY-WAND
Chamaelirium luteum

Lily family

Although it occurs in small, scattered colonies in several sections of the Smokies up to 2,500 feet elevation, this lily is rather uncommon. It grows along the Cades Cove Road, where it flowers in May and June. The white, curved flower-spikes appear at the top of stems 15 to 24 inches long. The plant is also known as RATTLESNAKE ROOT and DEVIL'S-BIT.

LITTLE BROWN JUG
Asarum arifolium

Birthwort family

Its arrow-shaped leaves and fleshy jug-shaped calyx—a flower without petals—give this plant a unique appeal. The thick, evergreen leaves are a familiar sight on wooded slopes up to 3,000 feet. Often hidden by the leaves, the interesting jugs occur at ground level, in May, and are purplish-brown and less than an inch long. Look for them along Sugarlands Nature Trail. Mountain children often pressed the fragrant leaves in their schoolbooks. Other names include PIGS, WILD GINGER, and HEART-LEAF.

CANADA MAYFLOWER
Maianthemum canadense

Lily family

This small herb, only 3 to 6 inches tall, is fairly abundant in moist, cool woodlands from 3,000 to 6,000 feet elevation. It flowers in June and July and occurs in the Heintooga Overlook and Andrews Bald areas. Another common name is WILD LILY-OF-THE-VALLEY.

WOOD ANEMONE
Anemone lancifolia

Buttercup family

The flower has no petals, but the white, petal-like sepals, occasionally tinged with pink, appear in April and May on plants up to 8 inches tall. Fairly common up to 3,000 feet elevation, it may be seen in moist, woodsy soil along the Abrams Falls Trail. This plant sometimes intergrades with *A. quinquefolia*.

Fairy-wand

Hutson photo

(left)
Little Brown Jug

Hutson photo

(right)
Canada Mayflower

Hutson photo

Wood Anemone

Macon photo

BASSWOOD   *Tilia heterophylla*
Linden family

These inconspicuous creamy white blossoms, suspended
from the convex side of a curved bract, are seen in June.
Bees turn to these flowers as an important source of honey.
Also known as LINN or LINDEN, the tree may be seen along
the Big Locust Nature Trail and along the road to Cades
Cove. Before the tree reaches maturity a dozen or so
young basswood sprouts appear around its base. A few
of these sprouts grow to maturity after the central, or
parent, tree dies. Resourceful early settlers twisted the
pliable inner bark from young basswoods to make rope
for their corded beds, for plow-lines and parts of harness.

POKEWEED   *Phytolacca americana*
Pokeweed family

This familiar and colorful plant, ranging up to 8 or 10
feet tall, flowers from May through September, often
showing ripe fruits at the same time. Pokeweed is widely
distributed in open areas of the lower park elevations.
The roots, mature stems, and interior of the hard-coated
seeds are very poisonous, but leaves and young stems
(not over 6 inches tall) are used as salads or boiled as
"greens." Its black, ripe fruits are used for making wine.
Another common name, INK-BERRY, was derived from the
early settlers' use of the fruit juice as ink. Locally it is
generally known as POKEBERRY.

NEW JERSEY TEA   *Ceanothus americanus*
Buckthorn family

Although early settlers used the leaves as a substitute for
tea, thereby giving its common name, this is not a member of the tea family. The low-growing shrub, also known
as RED ROOT, reaches a height of 2½ or 3 feet. It grows
abundantly at the lower elevations of the Smokies, and
may be found along the road to Cades Cove. The dense
clusters of flowers may be seen from May to August.

Basswood

Hutson photo

Pokeweed

Hutson photo

New Jersey Tea

Hutson photo

CARDINAL FLOWER
Lobelia cardinalis

Bluebell family

These brilliantly colored flowers are abundant at the edge of streams and in swampy soils up to about 2,500 feet. Watch for them in wet pasture areas along the Cades Cove Loop Road. They grow to a height of 3 to 5 feet, with flower clusters measuring 10 to 12 inches in length, and bloom from June through August. Four other lobelias, blue or purple in color, are found in the park.

GALAX
Galax aphylla

Diapensia family

This plant is more widely known for the beauty of its leaves, which turn copper-red in winter, than for its stately white spikes of flowers. It is abundant in dry woods up to 5,000 feet elevation, and may be seen along the Mids Branch Nature Trail. Galax is often called COLTSFOOT because of the shape of the leaves. The flower stem, seen in May and June, reaches a height of 10 to 15 inches.

CLINTON'S LILY
Clintonia umbellulata

Lily family

Two species of this rare lily, named for New York's first governor, are found in the Smokies. This white-flowered one is found only in the Southern Appalachians. In the Smokies it blooms in May at 2,000 to 3,000 feet, as between Cherokee Orchard and Rainbow Falls. The shiny blue fruits are quite attractive in August and September. The other species (yellow-flowered *C. borealis*) blooms in June mostly at higher elevations, as along the Spruce-Fir Nature Trail. Both species are also called BEAD LILY.

TOUCH-ME-NOT
Impatiens pallida

Touch-me-not family

Known also as PALE JEWEL WEED and SNAPWEED, this plant grows to a height of 3 to 5 feet in moist or wet soils at 2,000 to 3,500 feet. When the mature pods are touched, the fruits "explode," hence "touch-me-not." The related spotted jewel weed (*I. biflora*), usually at lower elevations, has orange flowers with brown spots. Both species bloom in July and August along Sugarlands Nature Trail.

Cardinal Flower   *Macon photo*

Galax   *Hutson photo*

Clinton's Lily   *Sharp photo*

Touch-me-not   *Hutson photo*

WILD GERANIUM *Geranium maculatum*
Geranium family

Pink to purple flowers appear in April and May on stems 12 to 18 inches tall. Because of its long, slender fruits, this geranium is sometimes called CRANESBILL. It is fairly common on wooded slopes up to 3,500 feet, such as along Sugarlands and Junglebrook Nature Trails and near Deep Creek Campground.

WILD GOLDEN-GLOW *Rudbeckia laciniata*
Composite family

The bright yellow flowers with short, cone-shaped centers occur on plants 3 to 6 feet tall at almost all elevations in the Smokies. One location is along the highway near Smokemont, where they flower from July to September. A related species, generally known as CONE FLOWER, has a more conspicuous cone.

WILD OATS *Uvularia sessilifolia*
Lily family

Also known as SMALL BELLWORT, the yellow, drooping flower appears on a stem 8 to 10 inches tall. Although widely distributed through lower elevations of the Smokies, it is seldom found in large numbers at any location. Several plants may be seen in April and May along the Pine-Oak Nature Trail.

MICHAUX'S SAXIFRAGE *Saxifraga michauxii*
Saxifrage family

Reddish-green leaves and stems—and spatulate leaves that are strongly toothed—help identify this species. Growing to a height of 10 to 12 inches, it prefers wet bluffs and boulders at elevations from 2,500 to 6,000 feet. In the vicinity of Alum Cave Bluff the flowers appear from late June through September. Another common name is LETTUCE SAXIFRAGE.

Wild Geranium   *Macon photo*

Wild Golden-glow   *Hutson photo*

Wild Oats   *Hutson photo*

Michaux's Saxifrage   *Macon photo*

ROSEBUD ORCHID
Cleistes divaricata

Orchid family

On rare occasions one may find this beautiful but uncommon orchid in the pine-oak forests in and near Cades Cove during June and July. The bronze-veined pink flower, up to 2 inches in length, occurs on stems from 8 to 24 inches tall. It is also known as SPREADING CREST ORCHID.

YELLOW FRINGED ORCHID
Habenaria ciliaris

Orchid family

The beautiful clusters of numerous small, fringed flowers, either yellow or orange, occur along the upper part of stems that range from 1 to 3 feet tall. Its habitat is acid, shady soils at elevations from 2,000 to 4,000 feet. Although widely scattered, this orchid may be found from July through August in pine woods near Cades Cove and along the road to Heintooga Overlook. It is closely related to purple fringed orchid (*H. psycodes*), which is shown on page 100.

GREAT MULLEIN
Verbascum thapsus

Figwort family

An introduced "weed," this plant became well established many years ago and is now a part of the landscape along roadsides and other open areas at the lower elevations of the Great Smokies. The scattered, small lemon-yellow flowers, seen from June through August, cover the upper half of stout stems which range from 2 to 6 feet high. Because of the presence of tight-growing woolly hairs, the leaves give the false appearance of being thick and meaty.

HAWKWEED
Hieracium pratense

Composite family

Masses of plants with yellow flowers in June and July add beauty to the shoulders and banks of the park roads to Clingmans Dome and to Heintooga Overlook. Six species of hawkweed, some of which are difficult to identify, are found in the Great Smokies.

Rosebud Orchid   *Sargent photo*

Yellow Fringed Orchid   *Hutson photo*

Great Mullein   *Hutson photo*

Hawkweed   *Hutson photo*

COMMON ELDERBERRY   *Sambucus canadensis*
Honeysuckle family

This shrub, 6 to 8 feet high, has big compound leaves on stems with extra large, pithy centers. It is the park's only shrub having compound leaves with white flowers arranged in large, flat clusters. Flowering in June and July, it may be seen in the vicinity of Sugarlands Visitor Center. The black fruits of common elderberry were used by early settlers for making pies, jellies, and wine.

TRUMPET CREEPER   *Campsis radicans*
Bignonia family

This low-growing vine is widespread throughout the low elevations of the Smokies and nearby foothills, where it is seen on roadside fences. The flower clusters, consisting of bright orange "trumpets" up to 3 inches long, are conspicuous from June through August. The compound leaves consist of 9 to 11 leaflets. When the plant is wet it is mildly poisonous to some people, hence another common name, COW-ITCH VINE.

RAMP   *Allium tricoccum*
Lily family

An annual festival near the Smokies is held to celebrate this "sweetest tasting, and foulest smelling, plant that grows." In early spring its tubers have a pleasant taste of sweet spring onions, but an obnoxious garlic-like odor persists for two or three days afterward. The broad leaves, resembling those of lily-of-the-valley, appear in April on moist, wooded slopes at elevations of 1,500 to 4,000 feet. Leaves disappear completely by late June, and greenish-purple flower clusters appear shortly afterward. In Northern states this plant is known as WILD LEEK.

Common Elderberry

Hutson photo

Trumpet Creeper

Thurmond photo

**(left)
Ramp leaves**

Hutson photo

**(right)
Ramp flower**

Hutson photo

PIPSISSEWA
Chimaphila maculata
Wintergreen family

This small evergreen shrub, 6 to 9 inches tall, is widely scattered in dry, acid woodlands up to 4,000 feet elevation and may be observed along the Cosby and Sugarlands Nature Trails. From one to three pendant flowers to a stem appear in May and June. Although the plant is also known as SPOTTED WINTERGREEN, its leaves have stripes rather than spots.

STIFF GENTIAN
Gentiana quinquefolia
Gentian family

Its profusion of flowers help distinguish this species from the other four gentians in the Smokies. As many as 50 flowers appear on each branched plant. The slightly "open" flowers, on plants 12 to 18 inches tall, range from violet-blue to lilac. They are plentiful along the road to Heintooga Overlook in August and September.

GREAT LOBELIA
Lobelia siphilitica
Bluebell family

Usually a deep, rich blue, this species occasionally may be pink or even white. The stiff stem is 2 to 3 feet in height, with flowers appearing in August and September. It is fairly common in moist locations at lower elevations of the park and is found in Cades Cove. The plant was once thought to be effective in the treatment of syphilis. Another park species, *L. inflata*, is used in preparations to curb the cigarette habit.

FALSE FOXGLOVE
Gerardia flava
Figwort family

Growing to about 3 feet tall, this stiff herb flowers in July and August. It is relatively abundant in dry woods at elevations up to 2,500 feet and may be seen along Sugarlands Nature Trail and in Cades Cove. Of the seven *Gerardia* species found in the Smokies, four have yellow flowers; the others are purple.

Pipsissewa   *Thurmond photo*

Stiff Gentian   *Hutson photo*

Great Lobelia   *Hutson photo*

False Foxglove   *Hutson photo*

CLOSED GENTIAN — *Gentiana linearis*
Gentian family

This rare narrow-leaved species grows on wet, rocky slopes from 5,000 to 6,000 feet elevation. Extremely rare south of Maryland, it is found along the Alum Cave Bluff Trail and alongside the Blue Ridge Parkway near the Smokies. It grows 12 to 15 inches tall and blooms in August and September. Its broad-leaved relative, *G. decora*, is fairly abundant in the park, especially along the Appalachian Trail between Clingmans Dome and Silers Bald. The bee that pollinates the closed gentian pulls the petals apart to enter.

GOLDENROD — *Solidago glomerata*
Composite family

This particular goldenrod, one of 18 goldenrods found in the Smokies, is both golden and rod-like. Species occuring at lower elevations have spreading flower clusters. This species is fairly abundant in a few open spaces at elevations of 5,000 to 6,000 feet, as on Thunderhead. Its usual height is about 3 feet, with flowers appearing in August and September. The heavy pollen of the goldenrods does not carry very far in the air, and seldom if ever causes hay fever. The ragweed, which blooms at the same time, is usually the hay fever culprit.

DOG-HOBBLE — *Leucothoë editorum*
Heath family

This arching 5 to 7-foot shrub usually grows in dense thickets in moist, shaded, acid soils from 900 to 5,000 feet. Dog-hobble is restricted to the Southern Appalachians. The strongly scented white flowers hang in clusters and appear in May and June. Its deciduous relative, *L. recurva*, is the only other species in the Smokies. In pre-park days, when bear hunting was practiced, the heavy bears could escape pursuing dogs by forcing their way through dense thickets of these shrubs, whereas the dogs became "hobbled" by the tangled growth. Look for this shrub along the Cosby Nature Trail or Cherokee Orchard-Roaring Fork Motor Nature Trail.

Closed Gentian

Hutson photo

Goldenrod

Hutson photo

Dog-hobble

Macon photo

EVENING PRIMROSE
Oenothera fruticosa
Evening Primrose family

The attractive yellow flowers with red buds appear from May to July on slightly branched plants about 2 feet tall. Fairly abundant on well-drained slopes and open woodlands from 1,800 to 5,000 feet elevation, it may be seen beside the road to Heintooga Overlook and along nearby portions of Blue Ridge Parkway.

ROSE-PINK
Sabatia angularis
Gentian family

Another common name for this flower, appropriately, is MEADOW BEAUTY. It flowers in August and September, and the angled stem may range from a few inches to 2 feet in height. Rose-pink is generally rare, but is fairly common in a few scattered, open areas having a sandy soil at elevations from 1,000 to 3,000 feet. It may be seen along the Cades Cove side of the Rich Mountain Road.

PASSION-FLOWER
Passiflora incarnata
Passion-flower family

Also known as WILD APRICOT and MAYPOP, this is a vine up to 10 feet in length. The unusual, fringed flowers are seen from June to September. Edible fruits mature from July into October. Its habitat is disturbed areas such as Cades Cove and Cherokee Orchard. This was Tennessee's State Flower until 1933 when the cultivated *Iris* replaced it. According to legend, the parts of the flower resemble the instruments of Christ's crucifixion—the corona representing the crown of thorns; the stamens and pistil, the nails of the cross; the petals and sepals, the faithful apostles. This and *P. lutea* are the park's only members of a large family of tropical plants.

Evening Primrose

Hutson photo

Rose-pink

Hutson photo

Passion-flower

Hutson photo

HAIRY BUTTERCUP   *Ranunculus hispidus*
Buttercup family

The beautiful yellow flowers, about one inch in diameter, on stems from 5 to 10 inches tall, occur mostly at elevations below 3,000 feet. They may be seen in the Little River Gorge from late March through April. Nine other buttercup species are found in the Great Smokies. All have distinctive shiny, waxy yellow petals.

PURPLE RHODODENDRON   *Rhododendron catawbiense*

Heath family

This gorgeous shrub, blooming in June and July, is one of the most popular wildflowers of the Smokies. Its rose-purple flowers are dramatic, and the shrub is easily seen because it grows well on exposed ridges at 3,000 to 6,600 feet elevation. The usual height is 8 to 12 feet, but occasionally it too attains the size of a small tree. Rhododendron is often intermingled with mountain laurel. Flower-clad ridges of these two shrubs are known to mountain people as laurel slicks and to botanists as heath balds. The dwarf rhododendron (*R. minus*) grows only 3 or 4 feet tall and is the only one of the three evergreen rhododendrons with short leaves (3 or 4 inches long).

WHITE RHODODENDRON *Rhododendron maximum*
Heath family

The white to shell-pink flowers of this species appear mostly in early July. It grows in deep forests, along streams, and in moist soils at all park elevations. ROSEBAY is another common name. Leaves of the plant thrown on a fire around which Indians are dancing are supposed to bring cold weather.

Hairy Buttercup

Hutson photo

Purple
Rhododendron

Hutson photo

White
Rhododendron

Hutson photo

WILD HYDRANGEA   *Hydrangea arborescens*
Saxifrage family

This wide-ranging shrub, 3 to 4 feet tall with many clusters of white flowers, is quite common on moist, shaded slopes from the park foothills up to 6,400 feet elevation. From May to August there are displays along both roads to Cades Cove. Widely distributed through the Southern Appalachians, the shrub is confused occasionally with some species of *Viburnum*.

SWEET SHRUB   *Calycanthus floridus*
Calycanthus family

Shrubs up to 6 or 8 feet tall bear a profusion of deep maroon or brownish flowers in May and June. Magnolia-like in form, the flowers are 1-1½ inches in diameter. This shrub usually has a spicy fragrance and is extremely variable, but most botanists agree there is only a single species. Found near Sugarlands Visitor Center and near Oconaluftee Ranger Station, it generally grows on stream banks and moist, wooded slopes at elevations below 3,500 feet. Other names are BUBBY-BUSH and CAROLINA ALLSPICE.

RED ELDERBERRY   *Sambucus pubens*
Honeysuckle family

Clusters of cream-colored to pink flowers, on shrubs 6 to 8 feet in height, appear in May and June—with bright coral or red fruits maturing in August. This species is fairly abundant in moist woods from 4,000 to 6,600 feet elevation, and may be seen along the park road to Clingmans Dome. Although inedible, fruits are not poisonous. A close relative, at lower elevations, is the common elderberry with black fruits.

Wild Hydrangea

Hutson photo

Sweet Shrub

Hutson photo

Red Elderberry

Macon photo

MOUNTAIN CAMELLIA
Stewartia ovata
Tea family

The large white flowers of this small tree, when seen from a distance, sometimes cause it to be mistaken for late flowering dogwood. It is quite rare, and the only member of the tea family in the Smokies. The mountain camellia blooms in June and is found in rich soils at 1,000 to 2,000 feet elevation. Near the Sugarlands Visitor Center are several mountain camellia trees.

WOOD SORREL
Oxalis montana
Wood Sorrel family

The small flowers with pink stripes grow on a low plant with shamrock-like leaves. It is abundant in the higher elevations, especially as a ground cover in the spruce-fir forests where it usually appears in beds of moss. There are five other species of sorrel in the park, all of which are also called SOUR GRASS. Wood sorrel is found along the Spruce-Fir Nature Trail. It flowers from May to July.

SERVICEBERRY
Amelanchier laevis
Rose family

The slender, white to pale pink petals with brown sepals appear as early as March in the foothills, with the flowering season advancing progressively up the mountain slopes. At elevations of 5,000 to 6,000 feet, blooms are found in late May and June. Most mountain people call it SARVIS, the Old English pronunciation for "service," and the plant is also known as SHADBUSH. The dark-red fruits, which are edible, ripen from May to August, depending on elevation. Serviceberry is abundant in Little River Gorge and in the Mile High area.

GRASS OF PARNASSUS
Parnassia asarifolia
Saxifrage family

Definitely not a grass despite its common name, this species is limited to the Southern Appalachians. In the Smokies it is found in moist or wet spots from 4,500 to 6,500 feet elevation, and may be seen on Mt. Le Conte. The white fluted petals have green stripes, appearing in August and September on stems 5 to 8 inches tall.

Mountain Camellia   *Hutson photo*

Wood Sorrel   *Hutson photo*

Serviceberry   *Macon photo*

Grass of Parnassus   *Hutson photo*

PROSTRATE BLUETS   *Houstonia serpyllifolia*
Madder family

The tiny flower is usually a rich, deep blue but occasionally may be light blue or even white. The plants are only 3 to 5 inches tall, with very small leaves. They are found in moist locations from 2,000 to 6,600 feet elevation and, because of their trailing nature, usually occur in dense beds. Prostrate bluets grow along the banks of the Clingmans Dome Road and in the vicinity of the Balsam Mountain Campground from May to August. Other common names are INNOCENCE and QUAKER MAIDS.

PURPLE BLUETS   *Houstonia purpurea*
Madder family

Usually 6 to 8 inches in height and with rather oval leaves, this tall *Houstonia* is fairly common on well-drained slopes from 1,000 to 5,500 feet elevation. The flowers, blooming from May to July, range from purple to lilac in color. They may be seen at Heintooga Overlook and at the lower edge of Andrews Bald. The plants are widely distributed through the eastern U. S.

BUTTERFLY-WEED   *Asclepias tuberosa*
Milkweed family

These orange-colored flowers are a conspicuous part of the landscape on dry soils in open areas up to about 2,000 feet elevation. They appear in Cades Cove and along the western end of the park from June through August. The stiff plant, up to about 2 feet high, is also known as CHIGGER WEED and ORANGE MILKWEED. There are five other milkweeds in the Smokies.

Prostrate Bluets

Hutson photo

Purple Bluets

Hutson photo

Butterfly-weed

Hutson photo

JACK-IN-THE-PULPIT   *Arisaema triphyllum*
Arum family

Easily recognized either by the unique "Jack" standing erect in his pulpit or by the one or two three-part leaves, this plant is widely distributed in the lower park elevations. From April to June it is found along Smokemont Nature Trail and at the start of Huskey Gap Trail. At the base of the "Jack" is a cluster of tiny flowers; a green or dark purple spathe forms the pulpit and curves over to provide a canopy. Another name is INDIAN TURNIP.

NORTH AMERICAN PAWPAW   *Asimina triloba*
Custard-apple family

The chocolate-brown flowers appear in April on trees up to 20 feet high. The edible fruits mature in August and September. Somewhat uncommon, the tree is found only in a few moist locations up to 2,500 feet. One thicket occurs between Gatlinburg and park headquarters and another above Smokemont. This is the park's only member of an important family of tropical fruits.

FALSE SOLOMON'S-SEAL   *Smilacina racemosa*
Lily family

The terminal flower cluster easily distinguishes this species from the true Solomon's-seal. Growing in areas below 3,500 feet, it is plentiful in Little River Gorge where the plume-like flowers appear from late April to June. The stems are 15 to 25 inches in height. Other common names include SOLOMON'S PLUME, SOLOMON'S ZIGZAG, and FALSE SPIKENARD.

SOLOMON'S-SEAL   *Polygonatum biflorum*
Lily family

This gracefully arching herb, usually 2 to 3 feet long, has greenish-yellow axillary flowers which appear in April and May. It grows on moist slopes below 3,000 feet elevation, occurring abundantly in Little River Gorge and along most of the nature trails.

Jack-in-the-Pulpit

Hutson photo

North American Pawpaw

Schiele photo

(left) False Solomon's-seal

Hutson photo

(right) Solomon's-seal

Hutson photo

GOAT'S-BEARD
Aruncus dioicus

Rose family

Creamy-white flowers, in plumes 3 to 5 inches in diameter and 6 to 10 inches in length, invite attention to this conspicuous plant, which grows 3 to 5 feet tall. It occurs at elevations up to 5,500 feet and may be seen along the park road to Heintooga Overlook, where the flower makes an attractive display in May and June. The male and female flowers appear on separate plants, but only the botanist is able to distinguish the difference.

SUMMER-SWEET
Clethra acuminata

White Alder family

A member of a tropical family, summer-sweet is a shrub that occasionally reaches 15 feet in height. In July and August, its numerous spikes of white flowers appear in Little River Gorge and elsewhere on moist slopes and along park streams from 1,500-5,500 feet elevation. Because early settlers used the dried seeds as a substitute for black pepper, they called it SWEET PEPPERBUSH. That, however, is a name applied by botanists to *C. alnifolia,* which grows on the coastal plains and not in the Smokies.

PURPLE WAKEROBIN
Trillium erectum

Lily family

In May and early June, the maroon or reddish-purple flowers of this *Trillium* add interest to the trailsides in moist woods of the high Smokies. It grows along the Spruce-Fir Nature Trail and elsewhere in the Canadian floral zone. Because of a slightly unpleasant odor, it is sometimes called STINKING WILLIE. The white form of this species, which is more abundant at lower park elevations, is shown on the back cover.

Goat's-beard

Hutson photo

Summer-sweet

Hutson photo

Purple Wakerobin

Hutson photo

PARTRIDGE-BERRY   *Mitchella repens*
Madder family

Very few flower species give us the opportunity to see brilliant fruits from last year, flowers of this year, and possibly even a young fruit from an earlier flower, all at the same time. (The picture at right is twice actual size.) Usually occurring in sizable beds, this small vine often provides a loose carpet in hemlock forests below 5,000 feet. The two tiny trumpet-shaped flowers with fuzzy petals grow side by side but produce only one twin fruit. These interesting flowers may be seen in May and June along the Cosby and Junglebrook Nature Trails.

TEABERRY   *Gaultheria procumbens*
Heath family

A tiny shrub, only 6 or 7 inches tall, the teaberry is prevalent in acid soils of oak and pine forests below 5,000 feet. It may be seen along the Smokemont and Sugarlands Nature Trails and on many of the heath balds of the mid-altitudes. Late June and July is the flowering season. Before the days of synthetics, this plant was a source of wintergreen (or teaberry) flavor. Other common names are CHECKERBERRY, WINTERGREEN, and MOUNTAIN TEA.

APPALACHIAN AVENS   *Geum radiatum*
Rose family

This extremely rare plant is restricted to a few high peaks of the Smokies and nearby mountains, where it flowers in July and August. Park regulations prohibit picking or otherwise disturbing all plants, but there is an additional reason for not tampering with this beautiful flower—its marked scarcity. The closest relative is Peck's avens of the White Mountains.

Partridge-berry

Heilman photo

Teaberry

Schiele photo

Appalachian Avens

Hutson photo

BLACK COHOSH
Cimicifuga americana
Buttercup family

The slender, wand-like clusters of white flowers, on plants 4 to 8 feet tall, have been described as "tapering candles to light Nature's church." They appear in June and July and are widely distributed at elevations up to 3,000 feet. They grow along the Big Locust Nature Trail and the Gregory Ridge Trail. Other common names include BLACK SNAKEROOT, RATTLETOP, and MOUNTAIN BUGBANE.

MOUNTAIN ST. JOHN'S-WORT *Hypericum graveolens*
St. John's-wort family

In the Smokies this yellow flower, which appears in July and August, is found only in the higher elevations. At 5,500 to 6,600 feet, such as on Mt. Le Conte and Clingmans Dome, it is fairly common. The plants are 15 to 18 inches in height. Some botanists insist that this species and *H. mitchellianum* are the same.

BEARD-TONGUE
Penstemon canescens
Figwort family

Clusters of light lavender or purple-striped flowers, on plants 12 to 18 inches tall, make attractive displays along park roads from April to July. Look for them in Cades Cove. Another species occurs at Mile High. The common name refers to a bearded, sterile stamen that appears in each flower.

INDIAN PAINTBRUSH
Castilleja coccinea
Figwort family

The showy color of this plant lies in the reddish-orange bracts, the bases of which are light green. Small tubular flowers, also light green in color, are almost hidden between layers of bracts. The plant, sometimes known as SCARLET PAINT-CUP, is 12 to 18 inches tall, with clusters of flowers and bracts about 1½ inches long. It may be seen near Mile High in June and July.

Black Cohosh   *Heilman photo*

Mountain St. John's-wort   *Thurmond photo*

Beard-tongue   *Hutson photo*

Indian Paintbrush   *Hutson photo*

MOUNTAIN ASH   *Pyrus americana*
Rose family

This small tree of the north woods, rare in the Smokies, is found this far south only at the higher elevations. It may be seen along the Clingmans Dome Road. Showy masses of white flowers appear in May and June, but the tree's greater beauty results from the shiny red fruits which appear in late August through October. The tree is so closely related to the apple tree, also of the rose family, that the two will sometimes hybridize.

CROSS VINE   *Bignonia capreolata*
Bignonia family

These golden-yellow, trumpet-shaped flowers with red centers are found from 1,000 to 2,500 feet elevation, late April—early May, especially in Little River Gorge. The tall, slender vines climb rock cliffs and trees alike, with flowers often seen 30 to 50 feet above ground. It is a representative of a large tropical family.

LADIES' TRESSES   *Spiranthes cernua*
Orchid family

One needs a magnifying glass to fully appreciate the beauty of the tiny white flowers arranged in spirals around the foot-high stem of this late-blooming orchid. It grows along the trails, such as the one to Laurel Falls, and in other relatively open spaces up to 6,000 feet. The flowers occur from August through October.

TURK'S-CAP LILY   *Lilium superbum*
Lily family

This showy lily of the high Smokies has orange-colored petals with brown spots. Several inverted flowers hang from supporting branches of stately plants that grow 6 to 10 feet tall. The leaves are in whorls about 10 inches apart. A large colony of this beautiful lily appears along the Appalachian Trail between Clingmans Dome and Silers Bald, where it blooms from July to August. It is related to the Carolina lily.

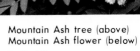

Mountain Ash tree (above)   *Hutson photo*
Mountain Ash flower (below)   *Schiele photo*

Cross Vine   *Macon photo*

Ladies' Tresses   *Macon photo*

Turk's-cap Lily   *Macon photo*

INDIAN-PIPE   *Monotropa uniflora*
Wintergreen family

An odd plant, without chlorophyll, Indian-pipe is found in thinly scattered clusters throughout the Smokies and may be seen from June through August along trails to Mt. Le Conte and beside the Spruce-Fir Nature Trail. The stem is 5 to 8 inches tall, with a single, nodding white or occasionally light pink or blue flower at the top. Another common name is GHOST PLANT.

PINESAP   *Monotropa hypopithys*
Wintergreen family

This non-green plant has several small, drooping, tan or red flowers at the end of a stem 5 to 8 inches tall. This is in contrast to the single flower of the related Indian-pipe. Fairly common in deciduous woods below 3,000 feet, pinesap is sometimes observed along the Pine-Oak Nature Trail, where it flowers from July to September.

GRASS-PINK   *Calopogon pulchellus*
Orchid family

This beautiful orchid grows to a height of 12 to 18 inches. A tall, slender, grass-like leaf reaches about the same length. Preferring moist, open areas at elevations from 1,500 to 4,500 feet, it occurs in the vicinity of Sugarlands Visitor Center and near Fontana Village. The flowering time is July.

FLY-POISON   *Amianthium muscaetoxicum*
Lily family

Moderately rare, fly-poison occurs at scattered park locations in open woods at elevations from 2,500 to 5,300 feet. It is abundant at Heintooga Picnic Area. The flowers appear in June and July on stems 2 to 3 feet tall. Arching basal leaves, with unusual V-shaped ribs, are 15 to 20 inches long. As the name implies, the plant has poisonous properties.

Indian-pipe   *Hutson photo*

Pinesap   *Hutson photo*

Grass-pink   *Hutson photo*

Fly-poison   *Macon Photo*

YARROW $Achillea\ millefolium$
Composite family

Flat clusters, about 3 inches in diameter, of white flower-heads appear in late May to July at widely scattered locations up to about 5,000 feet. Although an introduced "weed," only a few plants usually grow at any one site. Yarrow's small compound leaves are almost fern-like, and its stems are from 10 to 15 inches tall.

DAISY FLEABANE $Erigeron\ philadelphicus$
Composite family

With its head of yellow disc flowers surrounded by white (rarely pink) ray flowers, this plant resembles a miniature daisy. Eighteen to 30 inches tall, daisy fleabane is quite common at elevations from 1,000 to 2,500 feet. It may be seen along the Little River Gorge road below Elkmont, where it flowers from April through August. The plant was once used to repel fleas. A closely related spring species is robin's plantain ($E.\ pulchellus$), which has larger heads.

TRUMPET HONEYSUCKLE $Lonicera\ sempervirens$
Honeysuckle family

This slender woody vine, bearing the most brilliant of our honeysuckle flowers, occurs at lower elevations and on fences in nearby areas. It may be found in June along the road to Cherokee Orchard. CORAL HONEYSUCKLE is another common name, and locally it is also known as WOODBINE. It is not a vigorous pest like the Japanese honeysuckle.

VIRGIN'S BOWER $Clematis\ virginiana$
Buttercup family

Also known as COMMON CLEMATIS, this climbing vine, at times 30 or 40 feet long, is quite common in open areas at elevations up to about 2,000 feet. The numerous creamy white flowers abundant in July to September often almost obscure the foliage. In autumn the feathery fruits are almost as attractive as the blossoms. It may be seen in Cades Cove.

Yarrow *Hutson photo*

Daisy Fleabane *Hutson photo*

Trumpet Honeysuckle *Sargent photo*

Virgin's Bower *Thurmond photo*

NODDING POGONIA
Triphora trianthophora

Orchid family

This relatively rare orchid grows in moist, open, acid soils up to 3,500 feet elevation in the Great Smokies. The erect, branched stems, 6 to 10 inches tall, bear pink "nodding" flowers in mid-summer. A few of these flowers have been discovered near Cherokee Orchard and along the road to Heintooga Overlook.

LOOSESTRIFE
Lysimachia quadrifolia

Primrose family

The only loosestrife with whorled leaves in the Smokies is this species which is fairly common on dry slopes up to 5,000 feet elevation, such as at Mile High on the road to Heintooga Overlook. Flowers occur in July and August on plants ranging up to 3 feet tall. Another species in the park is *L. ciliata*.

RATTLESNAKE PLANTAIN
Goodyera pubescens

Orchid family

This orchid is characterized by its white-veined basal leaves peculiar to the genus. It has small white flowers in July and is found on moist, wooded slopes at elevations up to 4,000 feet, such as along the Cosby Nature Trail or between Cherokee Orchard and Rainbow Falls. Most stems, usually reaching a height of 10 to 15 inches, are considerably taller than the one shown here.

PURPLE GERARDIA
Gerardia purpurea

Figwort family

The flowers of this species so closely resemble those of two related species, *G. tenuifolia* and *G. setacea*, that a minute examination is necessary to distinguish them. Flowers of all three species may be seen in the meadows and edges of woodlands of Cades Cove, from August through October. The profusely branching plants, about 15 inches tall, are semiparasitic on grass roots.

90

Nodding Pogonia   *Hutson photo*

Loosestrife   *Hutson photo*

Rattlesnake Plantain   *Sargent photo*

Purple Gerardia   *Thurmond photo*

SWAMP-THISTLE — *Cirsium muticum*
Composite family

Large numbers of butterflies, especially black swallow-tails, are attracted to the numerous blue-purple flowers of this showy plant. The flowers, on branched plants 4 or 5 feet tall, appear from June into September. Swamp-thistle has very few spines. It may be seen in disturbed areas below 5,500 feet, as along the Mile High-Heintooga Road.

FILMY ANGELICA — *Angelica triquinata*
Parsley family

During late summer, this unique species is one of the most abundant and conspicuous wildflowers along the last 2 or 3 miles of the Clingmans Dome Road. Much of its interest lies in the complex form of the large clusters of flowers, on plants 3 to 5 feet in height. The plant warrants a close examination. It is probably poisonous.

COREOPSIS — *Coreopsis major*
Composite family

Also known as TICKSEED, this species grows to a height of about 3 feet and is common in open, well-drained park areas at elevations from 1,500 to 5,000 feet. It may be found in Little River Gorge, where it flowers from June to August. The leaves, which occur as opposite pairs, are so deeply cut that they resemble 6 whorled leaves.

Swamp-thistle

Hutson photo

Filmy Angelica

Hutson photo

Coreopsis

Hutson photo

BLACK-EYED SUSAN
Rudbeckia hirta
Composite family

This plant, conspicuous in flower, is one of five members of the genus in the Great Smokies. It may be seen at the edge of Indian Gap and elsewhere at elevations of 900 to 5,000 feet. Growing mostly on open slopes, the black-eyed susan reaches a height of about 3 feet, blooming in July and August. A closely related species is the wild golden glow (*R. laciniata*).

PURPLE-FLOWERING RASPBERRY
Rubus odoratus
Rose family

This gracefully arching shrub, with rose-purple flowers resembling single roses, reaches a curved length of 6 to 8 feet. In the Great Smokies it is found at elevations of 1,500 to 3,500 feet, but its range extends northward to Canada. The red fruits, highly acid and quite seedy, form a single layer around the central core—contributing another common name, THIMBLEBERRY. Early settlers often used the berries for making jam and jelly. There are two other raspberry species in the park. One of these, *R. idaeus* var. *canadensis*, also has red fruits, whereas *R. occidentalis* has black fruits. The purple flowers of *R. odoratus* appear near Chimneys Picnic Area from July to September.

CRIMSON BEE BALM
Monarda didyma
Mint family

Also called OSWEGO TEA, this bright-flowered mint usually occurs in beds of a few feet to several feet in diameter. It likes rich, wet, acid soils from 2,500 to 6,500 feet in elevation, and is quite showy near the entrance to Chimneys Picnic Area. The plant attains a height of 2 to 3 feet, and blooms in July and August. The leaves have a pleasant odor, as do those of the closely related bergamot (*M. fistulosa*) which has purple flowers.

Black-eyed Susan

Hutson photo

Purple-flowering Raspberry

Hutson photo

Crimson Bee Balm

Hutson photo

MONKSHOOD   *Aconitum uncinatum*

Buttercup family

In the Great Smokies the attractive and rare monkshood
is found mostly in open locations of the spruce-fir forests,
and may be seen on Mt. Le Conte. This species is restricted to the Southern Appalachians. The plants, which
prefer moist or wet soils, attain a curved length of 5 to 6
feet. Large numbers of blue-purple flowers bloom in August
and September.

PINK TURTLEHEAD   *Chelone lyoni*

Figwort family

A fairly abundant plant at higher elevations of the Smokies, turtlehead is not known to occur north of Tennessee
and North Carolina. It may be seen on Mt. Le Conte. The
stems reach a height of 15 to 24 inches. The shape of the
flowers, which appear in August and September, clearly
suggest the common name. If one will gently press the
sides of the flower, the "turtle's mouth" can be made to
open. Two related species, *C. glabra* and *C. chlorantha,*
also occur in the Smokies.

TROUT LILY   *Erythronium americanum*

Lily family

Few plants have such a widely accepted incorrect name,
often being called DOG-TOOTH VIOLET although a lily and
not a violet. The mottling of the 6 to 8-inch leaves suggest
the speckled trout of the mountain streams. Other common names include ADDER'S TONGUE and FAWN LILY. Trout
lily is widely distributed at lower elevations, but is sometimes found as high as 6,000 feet. The flowers, which appear in April and May, grow on stems 6 to 8 inches tall.
Cherokee Indians regarded the flowering season of this lily
as the time to fish for trout. It is found along the Big
Locust Nature Trail.

Monkshood

Hutson photo

Pink Turtlehead

Hutson photo

Trout Lily

Macon photo

JOE PYE WEED — *Eupatorium maculatum*
Composite family

"Weed" is the wrong name to apply to such a stately plant. Huge clusters of pink-purple flowers, atop coarse stems up to 12 or 15 feet high, are especially attractive, in both form and color, when seen against a blue sky. The flowering season is July through September. Cades Cove is a good place to view the plants, which like moist soils up to 3,000 feet. *E. dubium* and *E. purpureum* also grow in the park.

QUEEN ANNE'S LACE — *Daucus carota*
Parsley family

Also known as WILD CARROT, this plant is a familiar sight along roadsides and other disturbed areas of the park up to an elevation of about 4,000 feet. It may be seen in Cades Cove, where it blooms throughout the summer and early autumn. Most of the flowers are white, in flat heads or umbels, but on rare occasions they may be pale purple.

IRONWEED — *Vernonia noveboracensis*
Composite family

One of the park's most brilliant autumn flowers is produced by this impressive plant that grows 6 to 8 feet tall. Although rare generally in the Smokies, it is fairly common in disturbed areas below 2,000 feet. Flowering from August to October, this species is found in Cades Cove but in relatively few other locations. Another species, *V. altissima,* is quite abundant in open spaces of the park foothills.

Joe Pye Weed

Hutson photo

Queen Anne's Lace

Hutson photo

Ironweed

Macon photo

RUGEL'S INDIAN PLANTAIN   *Cacalia rugelia*
Composite family

Although not known to exist anywhere except in the high Smokies, this plant, formerly known as RUGEL'S RAGWORT, is locally abundant in the spruce-fir forests on peaks such as Mt. Le Conte and Clingmans Dome. The creamy-tan clusters of tiny flowers on plants up to 15 inches tall may be seen from June to September. The heads lack rays and are unusually large and compact. The split or bifurcated ends of each stigma curve in opposite directions.

PURPLE FRINGED ORCHID   *Habenaria psycodes*
Orchid family

Dozens of exquisite little orchids in clusters at the top of a 12- to 20-inch stem make this plant strikingly beautiful. Although not abundant, it occurs throughout the park in wet, acid soils at elevations of 2,500 to 6,500 feet. They may be seen in June and July along the road to Clingmans Dome.

CURTISS' ASTER   *Aster curtissii*
Composite family

This is one of the most abundant and most beautiful species of aster found in the Great Smokies. Flowers, ranging from white to rich blue, on stiff branched stems up to 3 feet tall, appear from late August to winter. Occurring in well-drained soils from 1,800 to 5,500 feet, they are plentiful in the vicinity of Mile High. Botanists find it difficult to identify positively many of the 18 aster species found in the park.

WHITE SNAKEROOT   *Eupatorium rugosum*
var. *roanense*
Composite family

One of about 12 kinds of snakeroot in the Smokies, this species is abundant on shaded slopes at elevations from 1,500 to 6,000 feet. From July to September it grows in profusion along the trail to Clingmans Dome Tower. The plants are 3 to 5 feet tall. Snakeroot is poisonous to cattle, and, through milk, to humans.

Rugel's Indian Plantain   *Hutson photo*

Purple Fringed Orchid   *Hutson photo*

Curtiss' Aster   *Hutson photo*

White Snakeroot   *Hutson photo*

UMBRELLA MAGNOLIA   *Magnolia tripetala*
Magnolia family

This is one of three magnolias native to the Smokies. All are deciduous. This species gets its name from the umbrella-like arrangement of the long leaves. The other two species are cucumber tree (*M. acuminata*) and Fraser magnolia (*M. fraseri*). The cucumber tree is so named because its large fruits resemble a cucumber. All three species are fairly common up to about 4,000 feet elevation. The cream-white flowers, which appear in April and May, are the park's largest flowers, some petals being 10 to 12 inches long. *M. tripetala* grows along the Junglebrook Nature Trail and in Little River Gorge.

HEARTS-A-BUSTIN'   *Euonymus americanus*
Staff-tree family

A beautiful shrub 5 to 10 feet tall, hearts-a-bustin' is found throughout the lower and intermediate elevations, usually near a stream. The early summer small flowers are inconspicuous, but the plant compels attention in early autumn when its wine-colored pods burst open, revealing brilliant orange-red seeds. Common names include STRAWBERRY BUSH, SWAMP DOGWOOD, SPINDLE BUSH, ARROWWOOD, WAHOO, and a dozen others. A relative, trailing wahoo (*E. obovatus*), is also found in the Smokies. The flowers or fruits of *E. americanus* may be seen along Sugarlands Nature Trail and near Oconaluftee Ranger Station.

WITCH HAZEL   *Hamamelis virginiana*
Witch Hazel family

From late October into January the cream-yellow petals of witch hazel are conspicuous along the streams in the lower elevations of the Smokies. The flowers are easily seen because they appear after defoliation of the witch hazel bushes. Since the flowers appear so late in the year, one might ask if this is really the last plant of the season to bloom. Perhaps it is first for the next season, since fruits resulting from these flowers do not develop until the following summer. Witch hazel is found in Little River Gorge.

Umbrella Magnolia
Macon photo

Hearts-a-bustin'
Macon photo

Witch Hazel
Macon photo

DOLL'S-EYES
Actaea pachypoda
Buttercup family

The interesting white fruits which mature in August and September get more attention than do the white flowers of late April and May. Not abundant, the plant grows to 2 feet tall in scattered locations up to 3,000 feet. It may be seen along the Sugarlands Nature Trail. Another common name is WHITE BANE BERRY.

HERCULES'-CLUB
Aralia spinosa
Ginseng family

The creamy-white flowers of July and August and the reddish-blue fruits of September and October are equally spectacular. A stout, thorny stem often rising to 15 feet is topped with a cluster of flowers up to 20 inches in diameter. Good displays of this shrub occur between Fighting Creek Gap and Sugarlands Visitor Center. Another common name is DEVIL'S WALKINGSTICK.

STAGHORN-SUMAC
Rhus typhina
Cashew family

This shrub, with a large core of pith, grows to a height of 6 to 10 feet and is plentiful up to 4,000 feet. Slender cones of greenish-white flowers appear in May, with fruits soon turning to a reddish-brown. Flower spikes are 8 to 12 inches long. The acid fruits were used by early settlers in making a cooling drink.

AMERICAN HOLLY
Ilex opaca
Holly family

This evergreen tree, with a spiny-margined leaf, is fairly common up to about 4,000 feet in the Smokies. Sometimes reaching a diameter of over 2 feet and a height of 80 to 90 feet, it may be seen along the Laurel Falls Trail. The small, creamy-white flowers of May and June are seldom noticed, but the tree is famous for its bright red fruits of autumn and early winter. Since the berries provide winter food for many birds, the use of twigs and berries for Christmas decorations is disturbing conservationists.

(left)
Doll's-eyes flower
Hutson photo

(right)
Doll's-eyes berry
Hutson photo

(left)
Hercules'-club
Hutson photo

(right)
Staghorn-sumac
Hutson photo

American Holly
Hutson photo

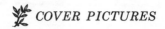 *COVER PICTURES*

MOUNTAIN LAUREL *Kalmia latifolia*
Heath family

(front cover) Laurel, a shrub which occasionally reaches the size of a small tree, thrives at elevations up to 5,000 feet, blooming in May on the lower slopes but from mid-June to July at the high elevations. A good way to distinguish laurel and rhododendron when not in flower is: "short leaf, short name; long leaf, long name." Early settlers knew laurel as ivy, and rhododendron as laurel.

FLOWERING DOGWOOD *Cornus florida*
Dogwood family

(back cover, top) One of the most familiar scenes in the Smokies—flowering dogwood in the foreground; Bull Head in the distance on the left and Balsam Point, the west end of Mt. Le Conte, on the right. (See also page 38.)

RUE ANEMONE *Anemonella thalictroides*
Buttercup family

(back cover, center) The delicate white flowers, on plants 6 to 8 inches tall, appear in April and May on wooded slopes up to 3,000 feet. Fairly abundant, they may be found along the Rich Mountain Road and along the Big Locust Nature Trail. The species is often confused with wood anemone, which has fewer and larger sepals. Neither has true petals, the sepals being petal-like.

WHITE ERECT TRILLIUM *Trillium erectum* forma *albiflorum*
Lily family

(back cover, bottom) This lovely white trillium, reaching a height of 10 to 12 inches, blooms in April and May. It is found from the foothills up to 5,500 feet elevation. There is a fine display at the upper end of the tunnel on the road to Cades Cove.

111

THE AUTHORS

CARLOS C. CAMPBELL, Knoxville, author of *Birth of a National Park in the Great Smoky Mountains*. While doing extensive hiking, the late Mr. Campbell was captivated by the floral variety of the Smokies and soon became an authority on both the history and natural beauties of the park. In recognition of his conservation activities he recieved the 1965 Horace Marden Albright Scenic Preservation Award of The American Scenic and Historic Preservation Society. Mr. Campbell and Dr. Aaron J. Sharp prepared the accompanying text.

WILLIAM F. HUTSON, M.D., radiologist, Chicago. Dr. Hutson, in pursuing his hobby of hiking and photography in the Great Smokies for more than 35 years, has built an extensive collection of wildflower color transparencies. A native of Tennessee, he is a graduate of The University of Tennessee, The University of North Carolina, and Northwestern Medical School. It was his love of the mountains that caused Dr. Hutson to initiate and make possible the publication of this book. His companion on most Smokies trips was Mr. Campbell.

AARON J. SHARP, Ph.D., Alumni Distinguished Professor of Botany, Emeritus, The University of Tennessee, Knoxville. This internationally known botanist knows the Smokies as do few others—from leading botanical field trips, conducting research, and hiking and camping out with his family. Dr. Sharp headed the U.T. botany department for 10 years but resigned from administrative duties to devote more time to research. He has completed and edited a checklist of more than 1,500 flowering plants of the Smokies, a project started years earlier by the late Dr. H. M. Jennison. Dr. Sharp collaborated with Carlos C. Campbell in writing the accompanying text.

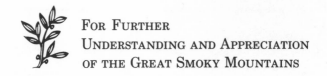

FOR FURTHER
UNDERSTANDING AND APPRECIATION
OF THE GREAT SMOKY MOUNTAINS

BIRTH OF A NATIONAL PARK
IN THE GREAT SMOKY MOUNTAINS
Carlos C. Campbell

Tracing the events that led to the establishment of the Great Smoky Mountains National Park, Campbell shows how the story behind the creation of the park is one of frustration, despair, political bias, and even physical violence. 184 pages, illustrations

THE GREAT SMOKY MOUNTAINS
Laura Thornborough

This volume shows why millions of people keep visiting the Great Smoky Mountains every year to discover new vistas, marvel at the variety of plant and animal life, and gain understanding and appreciation of the people who made the mountains their home. 224 pages, illustrations

A NATURALIST'S BLUE RIDGE PARKWAY
David T. Catlin

"*A Naturalist's Blue Ridge Parkway* is perfect for the sightseer and natural history student. The appendix provides checklists for ferns, wildflowers, trees, fish, amphibians, reptiles, birds, and mammals. This book should provide an extensive guide to the Parkway for the expert and novice alike."—*Virginia Wildlife*. 234 pages, illustrations, 12 in color

THE BLUE RIDGE PARKWAY
Harley E. Jolley

"Besides presenting a very readable, concise history of the Parkway with a well-chosen selection of photographs, Jolley has also provided a detailed bibliography and a thorough guide to the attractions along the route."—*Virginia Magazine of History and Biography*. 186 pages, illustrations